Let's Dance

Ballet Dancing

By Mark Thomas

Welcome Books

Children's Press
A Division of Grolier Publishing
New York / London / Hong Kong / Sydney
Danbury, Connecticut

Photo Credits: Cover and all photos by Maura Boruchow
Contributing Editor: Jeri Cipriano
Book Design: Michael DeLisio

Visit Children's Press on the Internet at:
http://publishing.grolier.com

Library of Congress Cataloging-in-Publication Data

Thomas, Mark, 1963-
   Ballet dancing / by Mark Thomas.
     p. cm. (Let's dance)
   Includes bibliographical references and index.
   ISBN 0-516-23142-1 (lib. bdg.) — ISBN 0-516-23067-0 (pbk.)
   1. Ballet—Juvenile literature. 2. Ballet dancing—Juvenile literature. [1. Ballet dancing.]
I. Title.

GV1787.5 .T53 2000
792.8—dc21

                                                            00-034632

Contents

My name is Tammy.

I like to dance ballet.

5

I go to ballet **practice** every Tuesday.

I have many friends in my ballet class.

7

We wear **leotards** for practice.

We wear tights, too.

Our teacher shows us
how to dance.

We watch as she moves.

Then we move as she moves.

11

We hold on to the **barre (bahr)**.

We bend our knees.

13

We point our toes.

We use our arms.

15

The class is getting ready for a ballet show.

We practice dancing on a **stage**.

17

We wear **costumes** for the show.

We wear **tutus** (**too-tooz**).

We smile at the end of the show.

We like to dance.

21

New Words

barre (**bahr**) a bar along a wall used for ballet practice

costumes (**kos**-toomz) clothes worn for a show

leotards (**lee**-uh-tahrdz) dance clothes that stretch for easy movement

practice (**prak**-tis) to do over and over

stage (**stayj**) a place where shows are put on

tutus (**too**-tooz) dance costumes with short skirts

To Find Out More

Books
ABC of Ballet
by Janet Grosser and Aline Ordmon
Dover Publishing

100 Lessons in Classical Ballet
by V.S. Kostrovitskaia
Limelight Editions

Web Site
Knowble
http://www.knowble.com
This site contains information about many topics, including ballet. In the ballet section, you can learn the history of ballet, play ballet games, and find out more about ballet dancing.

Index

About the Author
Mark Thomas is a writer and an educator who lives in Florida.

Reading Consultants
Kris Flynn, Coordinator, Small School District Literacy, The San Diego County
Office of Education

Shelly Forys, Certified Reading Recovery Specialist, W.J. Zahnow Elementary
School, Waterloo, IL

Peggy McNamara, Professor, Bank Street College of Education, Reading and
Literacy Program